CHAPTER ONE

PRIDE DEFINED: A BIBLICAL AND THEOLOGICAL EXAMINATION

Introduction: The Sin We Rarely Name

Among the sins addressed in Scripture, pride occupies a unique and dangerous position. Unlike overt transgressions—such as theft, immorality, or violence—pride often operates invisibly. It rarely announces itself as sin. Instead, it hides behind achievement, confidence, intelligence, spiritual maturity, leadership, and even moral uprightness. Pride is the sin most capable of convincing its host that it does not exist.

This subtlety is precisely what makes pride so destructive. Pride does not merely influence behavior; it shapes perception. It distorts how a person sees God, others, and himself. A proud individual may pray, serve, give, preach, and lead—yet remain fundamentally misaligned with God's purposes.

Scripture treats pride not as a personality trait but as a **spiritual condition of the heart**, one that provokes divine resistance.

"God resisted the proud, but giveth grace unto the humble."
— James 4:6

To be resisted by God is the most severe spiritual consequence imaginable. Grace is the divine resource that enables salvation, sanctification, calling, endurance, and fruitfulness. Pride blocks this resource at its source. Where pride rules, grace withdraws. Where grace is absent, purpose cannot be fulfilled.

This chapter seeks to define pride biblically and theologically, expose its spiritual mechanics, and establish why pride is not merely harmful but fundamentally **incompatible with God's design for human life**.

1. What Pride Is Not: Clearing Modern Confusion

Modern culture frequently confuses pride with healthy confidence, self-worth, or dignity. Scripture makes a critical distinction between **confidence rooted in God** and **self-exaltation rooted in autonomy**.

Biblical confidence is God-centered.
Pride is self-centered.

Paul models true confidence when he writes:

"I can do all things through Christ which strengthened me."
— Philippians 4:13

By contrast, pride removes God from the equation:

"My power and the might of mine hand hath gotten me this wealth."
— Deuteronomy 8:17

Confidence acknowledges God as source.
Pride credits self as source.

Pride is not simply feeling good about oneself; it is **locating one's sufficiency apart from God**. This distinction is crucial, because pride can coexist with outward humility, religious language, and moral discipline.

---

2. Biblical Language of Pride: Old and New Testament Insight

A. Old Testament Terms

In the Hebrew Scriptures, pride is often expressed through words that convey **height, elevation, and swelling**.

- **"Gābah"** — to be high, exalted, lifted up
- **"Zādôn"** — arrogance, presumption
- **"Rūm"** — self-exaltation

These words consistently associate pride with **self-elevation against God**.

"The LORD will destroy the house of the proud."
— Proverbs 15:25

Pride is portrayed not merely as an attitude but as a **posture of defiance**—a raising of self into a place reserved for God.

B. New Testament Language

In the Greek New Testament, pride appears as:

- **"Hyperēphania"** — arrogance, haughtiness
- **"Phusioō"** — to inflate, puff up

Paul warns the Corinthian church:

"Knowledge puffeth up, but charity edifieth."
— 1 Corinthians 8:1

The imagery is instructive: pride inflates without strengthening. It creates the illusion of size while hollowing substance. Pride expands the ego while weakening the soul.

---

3. Pride as Independence from God

At its core, pride is not merely self-love, it is **self-rule**. Pride declares independence from God's authority, wisdom, and timing.

This independence is expressed in several ways:

- Refusal to submit to God's Word
- Resistance to correction
- Trust in personal wisdom above divine instruction
- Desire for control rather than obedience

The prophet Jeremiah captures this condition succinctly:

"O LORD, I know that the way of man is not in himself."
— Jeremiah 10:23

Pride rejects this truth. It insists that man **can govern himself**, define morality, direct his steps, and achieve fulfillment without divine oversight. This belief is the theological root of rebellion.

4. Pride as the Sin Behind All Sin

While Scripture identifies many sins, pride stands apart as a **root sin**—one from which others grow.

- Pride precedes rebellion
- Pride precedes disobedience
- Pride precedes unbelief
- Pride precedes idolatry

The psalmist writes:

"The wicked, through the pride of his countenance, will not seek after God."
— Psalm 10:4

Notice the sequence: pride removes the need for God. Once God is no longer sought, moral collapse follows naturally. Pride does not always produce immediate scandal; it produces **distance from God**, and distance eventually produces destruction.

---

5. God's Posture Toward Pride

Scripture does not portray God as merely disapproving of pride. His posture is far stronger.

"Every one that is proud in heart is an abomination to the LORD."
— Proverbs 16:5

This language is severe. Pride is not listed among minor faults but among conditions God actively opposes.

The apostle Peter reiterates:

"God resisteth the proud."
— 1 Peter 5:5

The word *resisteth* implies opposition, obstruction, and warfare. God does not negotiate with pride. He resists it.

This is why pride is uniquely dangerous: **it places a person in opposition to God Himself**.

6. Pride and the Collapse of Purpose

Purpose flows from alignment. Alignment requires submission. Pride breaks submission and therefore disrupts purpose.

A gifted person may still fail.
A called person may still fall.
A chosen person may still be rejected.

Not because God withdraws purpose arbitrarily, but because pride **reorients the heart away from God's design**.

Scripture warns:

"Before destruction the heart of man is haughty."
— Proverbs 18:12

Destruction here is not limited to physical ruin. It includes:

- Moral collapse
- Spiritual dryness
- Relational breakdown
- Loss of divine favor
- Disqualification from calling

---

7. Pride's Most Dangerous Expression: Self-Deception

Perhaps pride's most lethal power is deception.

"The pride of thine heart hath deceived thee."
— Obadiah 1:3

The proud person rarely believes he is proud. Pride convinces its host that correction is unnecessary, that warnings are exaggerated, and that failure happens only to others.

This deception explains why pride often survives sermons, discipline, and even judgment—until collapse occurs.

8. The Antidote Introduced: Humility

Before Scripture ever commands humility, it reveals its necessity. Humility is not self-hatred; it is **truthful self-assessment before God**.

"Humble yourselves therefore under the mighty hand of God."
— 1 Peter 5:6

Humility restores alignment. It reopens access to grace. It repositions the heart beneath divine authority, where purpose can once again flourish.

Conclusion: A Foundation Laid

This chapter establishes the theological foundation for the entire work:
Pride is not a minor sin—it is a posture of independence that provokes divine resistance and destroys purpose.

Every subsequent chapter will demonstrate this truth in history, leadership, religion, and redemption. But before pride can be confronted externally, it must be examined internally.

End-of-Chapter Reflection

1. How does Scripture's definition of pride challenge common cultural views?
2. In what ways can pride exist without obvious arrogance?
3. Why does God actively resist pride rather than merely correct it?
4. Where might independence from God be quietly operating in your life?
5. What would genuine humility look like in your current season?

End-of-Chapter Prayer

Lord, search my heart. Expose every form of pride hidden within me. Teach me to walk humbly before You, that Your grace may flow freely and Your purpose be fulfilled in my life. Amen.

CHAPTER TWO

THE FIRST REBELLION: PRIDE IN THE HEAVENS

Introduction: Before Man Fell, Pride Had Already Fallen

Pride did not originate in the human heart. Long before Adam reached for forbidden fruit, pride had already corrupted a being of extraordinary privilege and authority. Scripture reveals that the first rebellion against God did not arise from weakness, ignorance, or oppression, but from **exaltation without submission**. Pride entered creation not through suffering, but through splendor.

Understanding the origin of pride in the heavens is essential for grasping its power on earth. Pride is not merely a human flaw; it is a **cosmic principle of rebellion**—a posture that seeks glory without God, authority without obedience, and elevation without surrender. What began in the heavenly realm would later be replicated in Eden and replayed throughout human history.

This chapter examines the fall of Lucifer, not as mythology or speculation, but as theological truth revealed through Scripture. It exposes pride as the first sin, the first rebellion, and the blueprint for all subsequent disobedience.

1. Lucifer Before the Fall: Privilege Without Precedent

The Bible offers two primary prophetic passages that, when read carefully, provide insight into Lucifer's original state: **Isaiah 14:12–15** and **Ezekiel 28:12–17**. While these texts address earthly kings (the king of Babylon and the king of Tyre), their language transcends human rulers and points to a supernatural reality behind them.

Ezekiel's description is especially revealing:

"Thou sealest up the sum, full of wisdom, and perfect in beauty."
— Ezekiel 28:12

Lucifer was not lacking. He was not oppressed. He was not ignorant. He was **full of wisdom** and **perfect in beauty**. Scripture continues:

"Thou hast been in Eden the garden of God; every precious stone was thy covering."
— Ezekiel 28:13

This description places Lucifer in proximity to God's presence, surrounded by glory and honor. He was not a marginal being but one entrusted with remarkable access.

Ezekiel further states:

"Thou art the anointed cherub that covereth; and I have set thee so."
— Ezekiel 28:14

The phrase *"that covereth"* suggests a role of proximity and protection near God's throne. Lucifer's position was not self-appointed; it was **granted by God**. His authority, beauty, and influence were gifts—not achievements.

This detail is crucial. Pride does not require lack; it often arises from abundance. The more gifted a being becomes, the greater the temptation to shift gratitude into entitlement.

---

2. The Nature of Lucifer's Sin: Self-Exaltation

Lucifer's fall was not caused by ignorance of God's greatness, but by a desire to **appropriate that greatness**. Isaiah records the internal declarations that defined his rebellion:

"For thou hast said in thine heart, I will ascend into heaven, I will exalt my throne above the stars of God... I will be like the most High."
— Isaiah 14:13–14

Five times Lucifer declares *"I will."* This repetition reveals the essence of pride: **the will of self-replacing the will of God**.

Lucifer did not deny God's existence. He sought to rival God's position. Pride does not begin with atheism; it begins with **self-enthronement**.

His sin was not ambition in itself, but ambition detached from submission. He desired elevation without obedience, authority without accountability, and glory without dependence.

3. Pride as Corrupted Worship

Lucifer's original role appears closely connected to worship. His beauty, wisdom, and position suggest that he was created to reflect God's glory, not to compete with it.

Ezekiel notes:

"Thou wast perfect in thy ways from the day that thou wast created, till iniquity was found in thee."
— Ezekiel 28:15

Iniquity here is not external transgression but **internal corruption**. Pride redirected worship inward. The creature began to admire itself rather than magnify its Creator.

This reveals a vital theological truth:
Pride is worship misdirected toward self.

When admiration of God diminishes, admiration of self-increases. Pride does not eliminate worship; it **reassigns it**.

4. The Moment Pride Crossed into Rebellion

Scripture tells us precisely what triggered Lucifer's fall:

"Thine heart was lifted up because of thy beauty, thou hast corrupted thy wisdom by reason of thy brightness."
— Ezekiel 28:17

Beauty did not corrupt Lucifer. Wisdom did not corrupt him. **Pride corrupted how he interpreted these gifts**.

The phrase *"heart was lifted up"* captures the posture of pride. His internal elevation preceded his external fall. Pride always begins invisibly, in the heart, long before consequences manifest.

Once pride took root, wisdom became distorted. Intelligence without humility produces arrogance. Insight without submission produces rebellion.

5. Divine Response: Expulsion, Not Negotiation

God did not reason with Lucifer's pride. He did not negotiate terms or offer compromise. Scripture is unequivocal:

"Yet thou shalt be brought down to hell, to the sides of the pit."
— Isaiah 14:15

And again:

"I will cast thee to the ground."
— Ezekiel 28:17

The severity of this response teaches an essential lesson:
God does not coexist with pride.

Lucifer was not gradually demoted; he was expelled. Pride cannot be rehabilitated—it must be removed. This sets the pattern for God's dealings with pride throughout Scripture.

---

6. From Lucifer to Satan: Pride's Final Transformation

Lucifer's pride did not merely cost him position; it transformed his identity. The one created to reflect God's glory became the adversary of God's purposes.

Jesus Himself affirms this event:

"I beheld Satan as lightning fall from heaven."
— Luke 10:18

Pride did not simply cause a fall; it produced **opposition**. The fallen cherub became the adversary, not because God created him so, but because pride reoriented his will against God.

This reveals pride's ultimate trajectory:
Pride turns servants into adversaries.

---

7. The Blueprint of Pride Established

Lucifer's fall establishes a pattern that will repeat itself throughout Scripture and history:

1. **Gift or privilege is received**
2. **Self-admiration replaces gratitude**
3. **Self-exaltation replaces submission**
4. **Rebellion follows**
5. **Divine resistance ensues**
6. **Purpose is lost**

This same pattern will reappear in Eden, in kings, in nations, and even in religious leaders.

---

8. Why This Matters for Humanity

Understanding pride's origin explains its persistence. Pride is not merely learned behavior; it is a **spiritual posture introduced into creation through rebellion**. When Satan tempted Eve, he did not invent a new strategy. He reused his own downfall:

"Ye shall be as gods."
— Genesis 3:5

The temptation offered to humanity mirrored Lucifer's original desire—to be like God without submission to God.

Conclusion: Pride's First Victim

Lucifer's fall reveals that pride is not a harmless flaw but a catastrophic force capable of destroying even the most exalted beings. If pride could corrupt an anointed cherub in the presence of God, it can certainly corrupt human hearts in a fallen world.

This chapter establishes a sobering truth:
Pride does not begin with rebellion; it ends with it.

End-of-Chapter Reflection

1. Why is pride more likely to arise from abundance than from lack?
2. How did Lucifer's gifts contribute to his downfall?
3. In what ways can worship subtly shift from God to self?
4. Why does God respond to pride with resistance rather than correction?
5. How does Lucifer's fall help explain the persistence of pride in humanity?

End-of-Chapter Prayer

Holy God, keep my heart from self-exaltation. Let every gift You have given me produce gratitude, not arrogance. Teach me to worship You rightly, that I may never trade purpose for pride. Amen.

CHAPTER THREE

EDEN REVISITED: PRIDE AS THE ROOT OF HUMAN SIN

Introduction: The Fall Was Not About Fruit

The fall of man is one of the most familiar narratives in Scripture, yet it is also one of the most misunderstood. Too often, the tragedy of Eden is reduced to a story about disobedience, appetite, or curiosity. But the sin in Eden was not primarily about eating forbidden fruit. It was about **authority, independence, and pride**.

Adam and Eve did not fall because they were weak; they fell because they were persuaded that they could live **independently of God**. Eden was not merely a garden—it was the environment of divine alignment. Within it, man enjoyed fellowship, authority, provision, and purpose. Pride shattered that alignment.

This chapter revisits Eden to expose pride not as one sin among many, but as the **root posture** that made human rebellion possible.

1. Man's Original Design: Authority Under Submission

God created man as a purposeful being, designed to function under divine authority. Adam was not created autonomously; he was created **dependent yet empowered**.

"And God said, Let us make man in our image, after our likeness: and let them have dominion."
— Genesis 1:26

Dominion was granted, but it was **delegated**, not inherent. Authority flowed from relationship. Man ruled the earth by remaining submitted to God's rule.

Genesis further clarifies this dependence:

"And the LORD God took the man and put him into the garden of Eden to dress it and to keep it."
— Genesis 2:15

Adam's assignment existed within boundaries. One command defined those boundaries:

"But of the tree of the knowledge of good and evil, thou shalt not eat of it."
— Genesis 2:17

This command was not arbitrary. It established a **moral boundary** that preserved man's submission. Obedience kept Adam aligned; disobedience would sever that alignment.

---

2. The Strategy of the Serpent: Reintroducing Pride

When the serpent appeared in Genesis 3, he did not introduce a new sin. He reintroduced the same posture that had caused his own fall.

"Yea, hath God said...?"
— Genesis 3:1

The first attack was not against obedience, but against **God's authority and credibility**. By questioning God's word, the serpent planted doubt. Doubt prepared the soil; pride would take root.

He then escalated the temptation:

"For God doth know that in the day ye eat thereof... ye shall be as gods, knowing good and evil."
— Genesis 3:5

This statement reveals the true temptation of Eden. The promise was not pleasure—it was **independence**. The serpent offered Adam and Eve the same lie that had destroyed him: *You can be like God without submitting to God.*

---

3. Moral Autonomy: Pride's Core Expression

The phrase *"knowing good and evil"* is often misunderstood. It does not refer merely to moral awareness; it refers to **moral autonomy**—the power to define right and wrong independently of God.

Before the fall:

- God defined truth
- God defined good

- God defined purpose

After the fall:

- Man sought to define these things himself

This shift marks the essence of pride. Pride is not simply self-admiration; it is **self-legislation**. It declares, *"I will decide for myself what is right."*

The prophet Isaiah later condemns this posture:

"Woe unto them that call evil good, and good evil."
— Isaiah 5:20

Eden was the birthplace of moral relativism, rooted in pride.

---

4. The Moment of Rebellion: When Pride Became Action

Genesis records the moment succinctly:

"And when the woman saw that the tree was good for food, and that it was pleasant to the eyes... she took of the fruit thereof and did eat."
— Genesis 3:6

Three elements converged:

1. **Desire** — "good for food"
2. **Attraction** — "pleasant to the eyes"
3. **Ambition** — "to make one wise"

These mirror the temptations later described by the apostle John:

"The lust of the flesh, and the lust of the eyes, and the pride of life."
— 1 John 2:16

Pride crowned the temptation. The act of eating was the external expression of an **internal decision**: man chose self-rule over submission.

---

5. Immediate Consequences: The Collapse of Alignment

The effects of pride were immediate and devastating.

A. Loss of Innocence and Peace

"And the eyes of them both were opened, and they knew that they were naked."
— Genesis 3:7

Awareness replaced innocence. Shame replaced peace.

B. Broken Fellowship

"And Adam and his wife hid themselves from the presence of the LORD God."
— Genesis 3:8

Pride always leads to separation. Once man asserted independence, intimacy with God became unbearable.

C. Shift from Responsibility to Blame

Adam blamed Eve.
Eve blamed the serpent.

Pride never accepts full responsibility. It deflects.

---

6. "Where Art Thou?" — God's Gracious Confrontation

God's question was not about location but **condition**:

"Where art thou?"
— Genesis 3:9

This was an invitation to repentance. But pride had already reshaped Adam's posture. Instead of confession, there was explanation. Instead of humility, there was justification.

The opportunity for immediate restoration was lost.

---

7. Theological Consequences of Pride in Eden

The fall introduced multiple layers of loss:

A. Loss of Glory

"For all have sinned and come short of the glory of God."
— Romans 3:23

Glory is the environment of purpose. When glory departed, clarity and direction followed.

B. Loss of Authority

Man's dominion became contested. Creation resisted him.

C. Introduction of Death

"For dust thou art, and unto dust shalt thou return."
— Genesis 3:19

Death was not merely physical—it was spiritual separation.

---

8. Pride Passed Down: The Generational Impact

Adam's pride did not end with him. It became embedded in human nature.

Paul explains:

"By one man sin entered into the world, and death by sin."
— Romans 5:12

Humanity inherited not only mortality but a **bent toward independence**. Pride became the default posture of the fallen heart.

This explains why pride appears universally across cultures, eras, and systems.

---

9. Eden as the Blueprint for All Future Rebellion

Every subsequent act of human rebellion echoes Eden:

- Nations defy God
- Kings exalt themselves
- People redefine morality
- Leaders resist correction

The pattern is consistent because the root is the same: **pride seeking autonomy from God**.

Conclusion: Pride Cost Man the Garden

Eden was lost not because God was harsh, but because pride was incompatible with paradise. A garden governed by self-rule would no longer be Eden.

This chapter establishes a sobering truth:
The greatest danger to human purpose is not ignorance or weakness, but prideful independence from God.

End-of-Chapter Reflection

1. Why was independence from God more dangerous than the act of eating the fruit?
2. How does moral autonomy continue to shape modern society?
3. In what ways does pride still manifest as resistance to God's authority?
4. How did pride immediately affect Adam's relationship with God and others?
5. Where might God be asking you, "Where art thou?" today?

End-of-Chapter Prayer

Father, forgive me for every desire to live independently of You. Restore in me a heart of obedience and humility. Let me never trade alignment with You for the illusion of autonomy. Amen.

CHAPTER FOUR

THE LOSS OF AUTHORITY: WHEN SUBMISSION ENDS

Introduction: Authority Is Not Self-Generated

Authority is one of the most desired yet most misunderstood realities in human life. People crave authority—in leadership, governance, family, institutions, and even spirituality, yet few understand its true source. Scripture is unambiguous: **authority does not originate in power, position, or personality**. Authority flows from **alignment with God**.

The fall of man was not merely the loss of innocence; it was the **collapse of delegated authority**. Adam did not lose authority because God arbitrarily revoked it, but because Adam severed the relationship through which authority functioned. Submission was the conduit. When submission ended, authority dissolved.

This chapter explores why **dominion without submission is impossible**, how pride dismantled man's authority, and why human attempts at self-rule inevitably produce disorder and bondage.

1. Dominion Theology: Authority as Delegation, Not Ownership

God's original mandate to humanity is often summarized in a single word: **dominion**.

"Let them have dominion over the fish of the sea, and over the fowl of the air, and over every living thing."
— Genesis 1:26

Dominion did not mean independence. It meant **delegated stewardship**. Adam ruled creation **on God's behalf**, not in his own right.

A critical principle is established here:

All legitimate authority is delegated authority.

Adam did not own the earth; he was entrusted with it. His authority depended entirely on his submission to the One who granted it.

Jesus later affirms this principle:

"All power is given unto me in heaven and in earth."
— Matthew 28:18

Even Christ speaks of authority as something **received**, not seized.

---

2. Submission as the Foundation of Authority

Submission is not weakness; it is alignment. In Scripture, submission positions a person under divine order, where authority can flow freely.

Consider the centurion's insight:

"For I am a man under authority, having soldiers under me."
— Matthew 8:9

Notice the order: **under authority before over authority**. This man understood a truth many leaders miss—authority only works when one is first submitted.

Adam's dominion functioned because he was **under God's authority**. The moment pride introduced self-rule, Adam stepped out from under divine covering. Authority cannot operate outside its source.

---

3. Pride as the Severing Agent

Pride does not attack authority directly; it attacks **submission**.

In Eden, Adam did not attempt to overthrow God openly. He simply chose to **act independently** of God's command. That act was enough.

"In the day that thou eatest thereof thou shalt surely die."
— Genesis 2:17

Death here was not merely physical—it was **relational and governmental**. Adam's authority was relationally sustained. When the relationship fractured, authority collapsed.

Pride declared, *"I will decide."*
Submission declares, *"God has decided."*

Where pride reigns, submission ends. Where submission ends, authority collapses.

4. Immediate Signs of Authority Loss

The loss of authority in Genesis 3 is evident almost immediately.

A. Creation No Longer Cooperates

Before the fall, creation responded to man effortlessly. After the fall:

"Cursed is the ground for thy sake… thorns also and thistles shall it bring forth."
— Genesis 3:17–18

The ground resisted Adam. Authority once exercised with ease now required struggle. This resistance was not punishment alone; it was **evidence of misalignment**.

B. Man Loses Mastery Over Himself

Adam could no longer govern his emotions, desires, or responses. Fear entered. Shame dominated. Self-control weakened.

Authority lost externally is always preceded by authority lost internally.

---

5. Chaos as the Natural Fruit of Self-Rule

When man rejected God's rule, he did not become free—he became fragmented.

Scripture repeatedly links self-rule with disorder:

"In those days there was no king in Israel: every man did that which was right in his own eyes."
— Judges 21:25

This verse does not celebrate freedom; it laments chaos. When everyone becomes their own authority, **truth dissolves, justice erodes, and confusion multiplies**.

Self-rule does not eliminate authority; it **multiplies conflicting authorities**.

---

6. The Illusion of Control

Pride promises control but delivers instability. The more humanity attempts to rule without God, the more disorder increases.

The prophet Jeremiah recognized this reality:

"O LORD, I know that the way of man is not in himself."
— Jeremiah 10:23

Self-rule ignores this truth. It assumes human wisdom is sufficient. History exposes the lie. Nations collapse, families fracture, and leaders fail—not for lack of power, but for lack of submission to divine order.

---

7. Authority Replaced by Domination

When true authority is lost, domination emerges.

Authority:

- Flows from alignment
- Produces peace
- Serves others

Domination:

- Flows from insecurity
- Produces fear
- Controls others

Pride cannot sustain authority, so it resorts to force. This explains why fallen systems rely on coercion rather than consent, fear rather than trust.

---

8. Spiritual Authority Versus Positional Authority

Scripture distinguishes between **positional authority** and **spiritual authority**.

Saul had a throne but lacked divine backing.
David had divine backing before he had a throne.

"Man looketh on the outward appearance, but the LORD looketh on the heart."
— 1 Samuel 16:7

Spiritual authority flows from alignment, not appointment. Pride may secure position, but humility sustains authority.

9. Christ Restores the Principle of Authority Through Submission

Jesus did not reclaim authority by asserting dominance, but by **perfect submission**.

"I seek not mine own will, but the will of the Father which hath sent me."
— John 5:30

Because Christ submitted fully, authority flowed completely.

"Even the winds and the sea obey him."
— Matthew 8:27

What Adam lost through pride, Christ restored through obedience.

10. Authority Today: Why Many Struggle to Lead

Many struggles with authority today at home, in ministry, in leadership because they seek authority without submission.

- Submission to God precedes authority over circumstances
- Submission to truth precedes authority in leadership
- Submission to discipline precedes authority in character

Pride skips submission and demands results. God does not honor that order.

Conclusion: Authority Cannot Survive Independence

This chapter establishes a foundational truth:
Authority is sustained only where submission is preserved.

Pride fractures submission.
Self-rule produces chaos.
Humility restores alignment.

Until submission is restored, authority will remain unstable.

End-of-Chapter Reflection

1. Why does authority flow from submission rather than force?
2. How did pride cause Adam to lose dominion without losing existence?
3. Where does modern society reflect the chaos of self-rule?
4. In what areas might you be seeking authority without alignment?
5. How does Christ redefine authority through obedience?

End-of-Chapter Prayer

Lord, teach me to submit fully to Your authority. Remove every trace of pride that resists Your order. Restore alignment in my life, that true authority may flow according to Your will. Amen.

CHAPTER FIVE

**THE GENERATIONAL NATURE OF PRIDE:

FROM PERSONAL REBELLION TO SYSTEMIC ARROGANCE**

Introduction: Pride Does Not Die with One Person

One of the most dangerous misconceptions about pride is the belief that it is purely personal; a private attitude confined to individual hearts. Scripture reveals a far more sobering reality. Pride, when left unrepented, does not remain isolated. It multiplies. It transfers. It institutionalizes.

Pride has a generational nature. What begins as a private posture of independence in one person can become a cultural norm in a family, a philosophy in a nation, and eventually a governing principle in institutions. When pride moves beyond the individual and becomes collective, it acquires momentum and legitimacy. At that point, it is no longer easily confronted, it is defended.

This chapter examines how pride travels across generations, how it embeds itself within societies, and why God repeatedly intervenes when pride becomes systemic. At the center of this discussion stands one of Scripture's most revealing episodes: **the Tower of Babel**.

---

1. Pride as a Transmitted Posture

While sin is not genetically inherited, Scripture teaches that **sinful patterns and postures are learned, reinforced, and normalized** across generations.

God warns Israel:

"Lest thou forget the LORD... and say in thine heart, my power and the might of mine hand hath gotten me this wealth."
— Deuteronomy 8:11–17

Notice that pride here is described not as an isolated thought, but as a **heart narrative,** a story people begin to tell themselves. Once internalized, this narrative becomes teachable, repeatable, and transferable.

Children learn pride not primarily through instruction, but through **modeling**:

- How authority is treated
- How correction is received
- How success is interpreted
- How failure is explained

Pride becomes generational when humility is absent.

---

2. Babel: The Birthplace of Collective Pride

The account of the Tower of Babel is the clearest biblical example of pride transitioning from individual rebellion to **collective arrogance**.

"And they said, Go to, let us build us a city and a tower, whose top may reach unto heaven; and let us make us a name."
— Genesis 11:4

Every phrase reveals pride's anatomy:

- **"Let us build"** — self-initiative without divine instruction
- **"Reach unto heaven"** — human aspiration replacing submission
- **"Let us make us a name"** — self-glorification

Babel was not an engineering project; it was a **theological statement**. Humanity was declaring independence from God on a civilizational scale.

This was not ignorance—God had already commanded mankind to **fill the earth**, not consolidate power in one place. Babel was deliberate defiance.

---

3. Pride as Fear Disguised as Ambition

Scripture reveals a hidden motive behind Babel:

"Lest we be scattered abroad upon the face of the whole earth."
— Genesis 11:4

Their pride was fueled by fear. They feared dispersion, loss of control, and dependence on God's promises. Pride often masquerades as ambition, but at its core lies **fear of trust**.

Rather than trust God's command to fill the earth, they chose to **secure themselves** through collective strength.

This exposes a profound truth:
Pride often emerges when trust in God diminishes.

---

4. God's Response to Systemic Pride

God's reaction to Babel is striking:

"And the LORD said, Behold, the people is one… and now nothing will be restrained from them."
— Genesis 11:6

This is not divine insecurity. It is divine concern. Unity without humility is dangerous. Collective pride accelerates rebellion.

God did not destroy Babel; He disrupted it.

"So, the LORD scattered them abroad… and they left off to build the city."
— Genesis 11:8

Scattering was mercy. God intervened to prevent pride from hardening into irreversible corruption.

---

5. Cultural Pride: When Sin Becomes Normal

When pride embeds itself into culture, it becomes **invisible**. Cultural pride does not feel rebellious, it feels normal.

Scripture warns Israel repeatedly:

"Say not thou in thine heart… for my righteousness the LORD hath brought me in."
— Deuteronomy 9:4

Cultural pride reframes blessing as entitlement. It interprets success as proof of superiority. Over time, humility is replaced by narrative, *we deserve this; we earned this; we are different.*

This is how pride becomes self-sustaining. Once normalized, it no longer feels sinful.

---

6. Pride in Nations and Institutions

Nations are not morally neutral. Scripture consistently holds nations accountable for pride.

"Righteousness exalteth a nation: but sin is a reproach to any people."
— Proverbs 14:34

When institutions operate without reference to God's authority, pride becomes policy. Systems begin to:

- Reward arrogance
- Marginalize humility
- Celebrate self-sufficiency
- Silence repentance

The prophets repeatedly pronounce judgment not just on individuals, but on **proud nations**.

"The pride of Israel testifieth to his face."
— Hosea 7:10

National pride becomes spiritual blindness when it resists correction.

---

7. Pride Passed Down Spiritually

The generational nature of pride explains why certain patterns persist across centuries:

- Repeated leadership failures
- Cycles of corruption
- Resistance to reform
- Persecution of truth-tellers

Jesus addressed this when confronting religious leaders:

"Ye build the tombs of the prophets... and say, If we had been in the days of our fathers, we would not have been partakers."
— Matthew 23:29–30

They inherited not just history, but **attitudes**—the same pride that rejected correction in previous generations.

---

8. Breaking the Generational Cycle

Scripture makes clear that generational pride is not irreversible.

"If my people... shall humble themselves."
— 2 Chronicles 7:14

Humility interrupts transmission. Repentance breaks cycles. God responds not to heritage, but to posture.

Individual humility can reverse generational arrogance.

---

9. Christ and the New Humanity

Where Babel unified humanity in pride, Christ reunified humanity in humility.

At Pentecost, languages were not confused but understood.

"Every man heard them speak in his own language."
— Acts 2:6

Pride divided. Humility united.

The gospel reverses Babel by restoring submission to God.

Conclusion: Pride Multiplies When Left Unchecked

This chapter reveals a sobering reality:
Pride is contagious.

Left unrepented, it spreads from hearts to homes, from homes to cultures, and from cultures to institutions. But humility—embraced sincerely—can reverse even generational rebellion.

God resists systemic pride not because He hates unity, but because He loves truth.

End-of-Chapter Reflection

1. How does pride move from individual hearts into collective systems?
2. What lessons does Babel teach about unity without humility?
3. How can fear disguise itself as ambition?
4. In what ways does cultural pride resist correction?
5. How can personal humility interrupt generational pride?

End-of-Chapter Prayer

God of mercy, forgive us for the pride we have inherited, normalized, and defended. Break every generational pattern of arrogance in our lives and communities. Restore humility, that Your purposes may stand. Amen.

CHAPTER SIX

SAUL: THE ANATOMY OF A REJECTED KING

Introduction: When Insecurity Wears the Crown

Few biblical figures illustrate the destructive complexity of pride more vividly than King Saul. His story is not merely about rebellion; it is about **unhealed insecurity masquerading as humility**, fear masquerading as caution, and pride masquerading as leadership. Saul did not begin as a villain. He began as a reluctant candidate, chosen by God, affirmed by prophecy, and empowered by the Spirit. Yet he ended as a rejected king—still anointed, still seated on the throne, but **abandoned by divine favor**.

Saul's tragedy warns leaders and believers alike that pride does not always announce itself with arrogance. Sometimes it hides behind fear of failure, craving for approval, and obsession with reputation. When insecurity is left unhealed, it often evolves into pride. And when pride governs leadership, rejection follows.

This chapter examines Saul's rise and fall to uncover how pride, subtle, defensive, and self-protective can dismantle divine purpose.

1. Saul's Calling: Chosen by God, Not by Ambition

Saul's ascent to kingship was initiated entirely by God.

"Tomorrow about this time I will send thee a man out of the land of Benjamin, and thou shalt anoint him to be captain over my people Israel."
— 1 Samuel 9:16

There is no evidence that Saul sought the throne. In fact, his initial posture appeared humble:

"Am not I a Benjamite, of the smallest of the tribes of Israel?"
— 1 Samuel 9:21

This humility, however, was **unexamined humility**—rooted more in self-doubt than in submission to God. Saul's sense of inadequacy was not healed by trust in God; it was merely suppressed by divine appointment.

Unhealed insecurity is not humility. It is vulnerability waiting to be exploited by pride.

---

2. Early Signs: Fear Before Faith

At Saul's public presentation, his insecurity surfaced immediately.

"When they sought him, he could not be found... behold, he hath hid himself among the stuff."
— 1 Samuel 10:21–22

This moment is often romanticized as humility. In reality, it revealed fear. Saul hid not because he trusted God, but because he feared exposure.

True humility steps forward in obedience.
False humility retreats to preserve self.

This pattern, fear leading to self-protection would later define Saul's leadership.

---

3. Pride's Early Camouflage: External Validation

Initially, Saul depended heavily on **public approval**. When victory came, he tolerated humility. When pressure mounted, insecurity surfaced.

Samuel warned Saul clearly:

"When thou wast little in thine own sight, wast thou not made the head of the tribes of Israel?"
— 1 Samuel 15:17

This statement is critical. Saul's downfall began when he stopped being "little" in his own sight—not because he grew in godly confidence, but because **his identity shifted from obedience to image**.

Pride does not always begin with self-love; it often begins with **self-preservation**.

4. The First Act of Disobedience: Impatience and Control

Saul's first major failure occurred during a military crisis.

"And Saul said, Bring hither a burnt offering… And as soon as he had made an end of offering… Samuel came."
— 1 Samuel 13:9–10

Saul's reasoning was pragmatic:

- The people were scattering
- The enemy was advancing
- Samuel was delayed

Under pressure, Saul chose **control over obedience**.

"I forced myself therefore, and offered a burnt offering."
— 1 Samuel 13:12

This confession reveals pride's logic: *circumstances justify disobedience*. Saul believed necessity overruled instruction. In doing so, he crossed a boundary God had clearly set.

Samuel's rebuke was devastating:

"Thou hast done foolishly… thy kingdom shall not continue."
— 1 Samuel 13:13–14

Pride convinced Saul that obedience was optional when inconvenient.

---

5. Partial Obedience: Pride's Favorite Compromise

Saul's defining failure came in his campaign against Amalek.

"Now go and smite Amalek, and utterly destroy all that they have."
— 1 Samuel 15:3

The command was explicit. Saul's response was selective.

"But Saul and the people spared Agag, and the best of the sheep."
— 1 Samuel 15:9

Partial obedience is not obedience—it is **rebranded disobedience**. Saul rationalized his actions as religious sacrifice.

Samuel's response exposes the heart of the matter:

"To obey is better than sacrifice."
— 1 Samuel 15:22

Saul's pride preferred **appearance over alignment**. He wanted to look obedient without fully surrendering control.

---

6. Pride Exposed: Fear of People Over Fear of God

When confronted, Saul revealed the true source of his behavior:

"I feared the people, and obeyed their voice."
— 1 Samuel 15:24

Fear of people is a subtle form of pride. It elevates human opinion above divine command. Saul's leadership was governed by polls, pressure, and perception—not by obedience.

Pride seeks approval.
Humility seeks alignment.

---

7. The Tragedy of Rejection

Samuel's pronouncement was final:

"The LORD hath rejected thee from being king."
— 1 Samuel 15:26

This rejection did not remove Saul immediately from the throne. Instead, it removed **God's presence**.

"The Spirit of the LORD departed from Saul."
— 1 Samuel 16:14

This is the most terrifying consequence of pride: **to continue functioning without divine endorsement**.

Saul still wore the crown.
But heaven had moved on.

---

8. Pride After Rejection: From Insecurity to Paranoia

Once rejected, Saul's insecurity mutated into paranoia. David's success threatened Saul's identity.

"Saul hath slain his thousands, and David his ten thousands."
— 1 Samuel 18:7

Saul responded with jealousy, rage, and obsession.

Pride that is unrepented becomes destructive. What began as fear of failure became fear of replacement. Saul's leadership devolved into self-defense.

---

9. Saul and David: A Tale of Two Hearts

Saul and David both sinned. The difference was not morality, it was **posture**.

- Saul defended himself
- David confessed
- Saul blamed others
- David took responsibility

"A broken and a contrite heart, O God, thou wilt not despise."
— Psalm 51:17

Pride disqualifies not because of failure, but because of **refusal to repent**.

---

10. Leadership Lessons from Saul

Saul's life teaches sobering truths:

- Insecurity can evolve into pride
- Pressure exposes posture

- Partial obedience is rebellion
- Fear of people undermines authority
- Pride resists repentance

Leadership without humility is unsustainable.

Conclusion: The Cost of Preserving Self

Saul lost his kingdom not because he lacked ability, but because he lacked surrender. He chose self-preservation over submission, reputation over repentance, and control over obedience.

This chapter establishes a hard truth:
God can work with weakness, but He resists pride—even when it wears a crown.

End-of-Chapter Reflection

1. How can insecurity masquerade as humility?
2. Why is partial obedience more dangerous than open rebellion?
3. How does fear of people undermine spiritual authority?
4. What distinguishes Saul's response to failure from David's?
5. Where might God be calling you from self-preservation to surrender?

End-of-Chapter Prayer

Lord, heal every insecurity that competes with obedience in my heart. Deliver me from the pride that seeks approval over alignment. Give me a heart that repents quickly and obeys fully. Amen.

CHAPTER SEVEN

PHARAOH: HARDENED BY PRIDE

Introduction: When Power Refuses to Bow

Few figures in Scripture embody the catastrophic consequences of pride in leadership as clearly as Pharaoh, king of Egypt. Pharaoh was not merely an individual ruler; he was the embodiment of a system, a culture, and a worldview that exalted human power above divine authority. His pride was not hidden, it was public, institutionalized, and aggressively defended.

Pharaoh's story confronts one of the most unsettling realities in Scripture: **a heart that becomes hardened through repeated resistance to God**. This hardening does not occur suddenly. It is progressive. It begins with delay, moves to defiance, and culminates in destruction. At every stage, Pharaoh had opportunities to repent. Pride ensured he refused them.

This chapter explores how pride hardens the heart, how delayed obedience becomes disobedience, and why arrogant leadership never collapses alone, it takes nations with it.

1. Pharaoh's Worldview: Power Without Accountability

To understand Pharaoh's pride, one must understand his worldview. Pharaoh was not merely a political ruler; in Egyptian theology, he was regarded as **divine**. He was believed to be the son of the gods, the mediator between heaven and earth, and the guarantor of order.

This belief system made Pharaoh resistant to any authority above himself.

When Moses first confronted him with God's command, Pharaoh responded with a question that exposed the core of his pride:

"Who is the LORD, that I should obey his voice?"
— Exodus 5:2

This was not ignorance, it was defiance. Pharaoh was not asking to learn; he was declaring independence. Pride does not seek understanding; it asserts superiority.

2. Pride's First Defense: Denial and Dismissal

Pharaoh's initial response to God's command was dismissal. He neither investigated nor reflected. He immediately rejected the claim.

This pattern reveals pride's first line of defense: **dismissal of authority it does not recognize**.

Instead of releasing Israel, Pharaoh increased their labor:

"Let the work be heavier upon the men."
— Exodus 5:9

Pride often responds to conviction by tightening control. Rather than soften, Pharaoh hardened his stance, believing pressure would silence opposition.

---

3. The Hardening of the Heart: A Progressive Process

The book of Exodus repeatedly references Pharaoh's hardened heart. This concept has generated theological debate, but Scripture presents a consistent pattern.

At first, Pharaoh hardened his own heart:

"And Pharaoh's heart was hardened."
— Exodus 7:13

Later, Scripture states:

"The LORD hardened Pharaoh's heart."
— Exodus 9:12

This progression is critical. God did not harden Pharaoh's heart arbitrarily. Pharaoh repeatedly resisted truth until his heart became **judicially hardened**, confirmed in the posture he had chosen.

Hardening is not the removal of opportunity; it is the **confirmation of resistance**.

---

4. Delayed Obedience: The Subtle Form of Pride

Pharaoh occasionally appeared to relent.

"I have sinned this time: the LORD is righteous."
— Exodus 9:27

Yet these admissions were always temporary. Once pressure lifted, Pharaoh reverted.

"When Pharaoh saw that the rain and the hail... were ceased, he sinned yet more, and hardened his heart."
— Exodus 9:34

Delayed obedience is pride's compromise. It acknowledges truth without surrendering to it. Pharaoh wanted relief without repentance.

Pride often says, *"Later,"* when God says, *"Now."*

---

5. Signs and Wonders: Mercy Before Judgment

Each plague was not merely punishment—it was **an opportunity for repentance**. God escalated gradually, allowing Pharaoh repeated chances to humble himself.

The plagues dismantled Egypt's gods one by one:

- The Nile
- Frogs
- Darkness
- Livestock
- The sun god

God was exposing Egypt's false sources of power. Pride resists even when false foundations are clearly revealed.

---

6. The Cost of Arrogant Leadership

Pharaoh's pride did not remain personal. His refusal affected an entire nation.

- Economic collapse
- Agricultural devastation
- Social instability

- National mourning

"There was not a house where there was not one dead."
— Exodus 12:30

Arrogant leadership always exports suffering. Pharaoh's pride became Egypt's grief.

This reveals a sobering truth:
Leadership pride multiplies consequences.

---

7. The Final Act of Pride: Regret Without Repentance

Even after releasing Israel, Pharaoh's pride resurfaced.

"Why have we done this, that we have let Israel go from serving us?"
— Exodus 14:5

Pride regretted loss of control, not rebellion against God. Pharaoh pursued Israel into the Red Sea—not to repent, but to reclaim dominance.

The result was final:

"The waters returned… there remained not so much as one of them."
— Exodus 14:28

Pride that refuses to repent eventually meets irreversible judgment.

---

8. Pharaoh as a Warning to Leaders and Nations

Paul later reflects on Pharaoh's story:

"Even for this same purpose have I raised thee up, that I might shew my power in thee."
— Romans 9:17

This does not mean God created Pharaoh to be evil. It means God **used Pharaoh's chosen posture** to display divine sovereignty.

Pharaoh stands as a warning:

- Power does not exempt one from accountability
- Delay does not equal obedience

- Pride does not negotiate outcomes

9. Pride Versus the Fear of the Lord

The contrast in Exodus is stark. While Pharaoh hardened his heart, some Egyptians humbled themselves:

"He that feared the word of the LORD among the servants of Pharaoh made his servants and his cattle flee."
— Exodus 9:20

Humility always preserves life. Pride endangers it.

10. Lessons for the Modern World

Pharaoh's story is not ancient history alone—it is timeless theology. Whenever leaders:

- Silence truth
- Resist correction
- Delay obedience
- Preserve power at all costs

They reenact Pharaoh's error.

God remains patient—but patience is not permission.

Conclusion: When the Heart Will Not Yield

Pharaoh's downfall was not due to lack of evidence but refusal to yield. Pride hardened his heart until repentance was no longer possible.

This chapter teaches a sobering truth:
A hardened heart is not formed by one act of rebellion, but by repeated resistance to truth.

End-of-Chapter Reflection

1. How did Pharaoh's worldview contribute to his resistance to God?
2. Why is delayed obedience a form of pride?
3. How does repeated resistance lead to hardened hearts?
4. In what ways does leadership pride affect others?
5. Where might God be calling you to respond now rather than later?

End-of-Chapter Prayer

Merciful God, soften my heart toward Your truth. Deliver me from pride that delays obedience. Teach me to yield quickly, that I may never harden my heart against You. Amen.

CHAPTER EIGHT

NEBUCHADNEZZAR: DISCIPLINED, NOT DESTROYED

Introduction: When God Interrupts Pride with Mercy

Not all encounters between pride and divine judgment end in destruction. While some leaders harden themselves until repentance becomes impossible, others are humbled, corrected, and restored. The story of King Nebuchadnezzar stands as one of Scripture's clearest testimonies that **God disciplines the proud in order to save them**, not simply to shame them.

Nebuchadnezzar was among the most powerful rulers in human history. He conquered nations, reshaped civilizations, and presided over an empire unmatched in scale and splendor. Yet his greatest threat was not military opposition—it was **his own pride**. Unlike Pharaoh, Nebuchadnezzar was not destroyed. He was disciplined. And through discipline, he came to know the sovereignty of God.

This chapter explores the difference between **judgment and discipline**, the purpose of divine humiliation, and the mercy embedded in God's correction of pride.

1. Nebuchadnezzar's Rise: Power as a Test of the Heart

Nebuchadnezzar did not seize power unlawfully. Scripture explicitly affirms that his authority was **permitted by God**.

"Thou, O king, art a king of kings: for the God of heaven hath given thee a kingdom, power, and strength, and glory."
— Daniel 2:37

This declaration is crucial. Nebuchadnezzar's greatness was not self-generated. It was **delegated**. His empire existed by divine allowance, not human brilliance alone.

Yet power, when unaccompanied by humility, becomes a spiritual test. Success reveals the heart more thoroughly than adversity. It was not Nebuchadnezzar's weakness that endangered him, but his **unchecked prosperity**.

2. Pride Revealed: The Language of Self-Glory

Nebuchadnezzar's pride reached its peak in a single, revealing declaration:

"Is not this great Babylon, that I have built for the house of the kingdom by the might of my power, and for the honour of my majesty?"
— Daniel 4:30

This statement encapsulates pride's essence:

- **"I have built"** — self-credit
- **"My power"** — self-sufficiency
- **"My majesty"** — self-glorification

God was entirely absent from Nebuchadnezzar's narrative. Pride rewrites history to exclude divine involvement.

---

3. God's Warning: Mercy Before Discipline

Unlike Pharaoh, Nebuchadnezzar received **advance warning**. God did not ambush him with judgment; He appealed to him through a troubling dream.

Daniel faithfully interpreted the dream and issued a clear call to repentance:

"Break off thy sins by righteousness, and thine iniquities by shewing mercy to the poor."
— Daniel 4:27

This verse reveals God's heart. Discipline was **conditional**, not inevitable. Repentance could have altered the outcome.

The delay of twelve months between the warning and the judgment demonstrates divine patience. God gave Nebuchadnezzar time to humble himself.

Pride ignored the warning.

---

4. Divine Discipline Defined: Correction, Not Condemnation

When judgment finally came, it was severe but purposeful.

"They shall drive thee from men, and thy dwelling shall be with the beasts of the field."
— Daniel 4:32

Nebuchadnezzar lost:

- His throne
- His dignity
- His sanity

Yet he did not lose his life.

This distinction matters. Discipline is not annihilation. It is **intervention designed to restore alignment**.

The writer of Hebrews explains:

"For whom the Lord loveth he chasteneth."
— Hebrews 12:6

Nebuchadnezzar's humiliation was evidence not of abandonment, but of divine concern.

---

5. Humiliation as a Pathway to Humility

For seven years, Nebuchadnezzar lived like an animal. The king who exalted himself above men was reduced below them.

This humiliation reversed pride's distortion. Pride elevates self above reality. Humiliation restores truth.

"Till thou know that the most High ruleth in the kingdom of men."
— Daniel 4:32

God's objective was not suffering—it was **knowledge of sovereignty**.

Humility is often learned when illusion collapses.

6. The Turning Point: Recognition of God's Authority

The restoration of Nebuchadnezzar began with a single act: **acknowledgment**.

"And at the end of the days I Nebuchadnezzar lifted up mine eyes unto heaven."
— Daniel 4:34

This upward gaze symbolized surrender. Pride looks inward. Humility looks upward.

Immediately, understanding returned:

"And mine understanding returned unto me."
— Daniel 4:34

Restoration followed recognition.

---

7. Praise Replaces Pride

Nebuchadnezzar's transformation was not superficial. His confession was theological, not emotional:

"All the inhabitants of the earth are reputed as nothing: and he doeth according to his will."
— Daniel 4:35

The king who once exalted himself now exalted God. Pride had been replaced with reverence.

True humility does not diminish leadership, it **redeems it**.

---

8. Restoration Without Resentment

Scripture records an extraordinary outcome:

"My reason returned unto me; and for the glory of my kingdom... my counsellors and my lords sought unto me."
— Daniel 4:36

Nebuchadnezzar was restored fully:

- His throne
- His honor

- His influence

God did not permanently disqualify him. He corrected him.

This reveals a vital truth:

God opposes pride but restores the humble.

---

9. Discipline Versus Destruction: A Theological Contrast

Comparing Pharaoh and Nebuchadnezzar is instructive:

- Pharaoh hardened himself and was destroyed
- Nebuchadnezzar humbled himself and was restored

The difference was not God's power, but **human response**.

Pride that resists correction leads to judgment.
Pride that yields under correction leads to restoration.

---

10. Lessons for Leaders and Believers

Nebuchadnezzar's story offers enduring lessons:

- Success is a spiritual test
- God warns before He disciplines
- Humiliation can be redemptive
- Restoration follows surrender

Leadership does not exempt anyone from accountability. But humility can preserve both calling and legacy.

Conclusion: The Mercy Hidden in Discipline

Nebuchadnezzar's story reveals a God who disciplines not to destroy, but to save. Pride was confronted, stripped, and replaced—not by annihilation, but by mercy.

This chapter teaches a powerful truth:
God's discipline is severe only because His purpose is restorative.

End-of-Chapter Reflection

1. Why is success often a greater spiritual test than hardship?
2. How does God demonstrate mercy even in severe discipline?
3. What role does humility play in restoration?
4. How does Nebuchadnezzar's response differ from Pharaoh's?
5. Where might God be warning you before discipline becomes necessary?

End-of-Chapter Prayer

Sovereign Lord, keep my heart humble in seasons of success. Teach me to heed Your warnings and submit to Your authority. Let discipline produce righteousness and restoration in my life. Amen.

CHAPTER EIGHT

NEBUCHADNEZZAR: DISCIPLINED, NOT DESTROYED

Introduction: When God Interrupts Pride with Mercy

Not all encounters between pride and divine judgment end in destruction. While some leaders harden themselves until repentance becomes impossible, others are humbled, corrected, and restored. The story of King Nebuchadnezzar stands as one of Scripture's clearest testimonies that **God disciplines the proud in order to save them**, not simply to shame them.

Nebuchadnezzar was among the most powerful rulers in human history. He conquered nations, reshaped civilizations, and presided over an empire unmatched in scale and splendor. Yet his greatest threat was not military opposition, it was **his own pride**. Unlike Pharaoh, Nebuchadnezzar was not destroyed. He was disciplined. And through discipline, he came to know the sovereignty of God.

This chapter explores the difference between **judgment and discipline**, the purpose of divine humiliation, and the mercy embedded in God's correction of pride.

1. Nebuchadnezzar's Rise: Power as a Test of the Heart

Nebuchadnezzar did not seize power unlawfully. Scripture explicitly affirms that his authority was **permitted by God**.

"Thou, O king, art a king of kings: for the God of heaven hath given thee a kingdom, power, and strength, and glory."
— Daniel 2:37

This declaration is crucial. Nebuchadnezzar's greatness was not self-generated. It was **delegated**. His empire existed by divine allowance, not human brilliance alone.

Yet power, when unaccompanied by humility, becomes a spiritual test. Success reveals the heart more thoroughly than adversity. It was not Nebuchadnezzar's weakness that endangered him, but his **unchecked prosperity**.

2. Pride Revealed: The Language of Self-Glory

Nebuchadnezzar's pride reached its peak in a single, revealing declaration:

"Is not this great Babylon, that I have built for the house of the kingdom by the might of my power, and for the honour of my majesty?"
— Daniel 4:30

This statement encapsulates pride's essence:

- **"I have built"** — self-credit
- **"My power"** — self-sufficiency
- **"My majesty"** — self-glorification

God was entirely absent from Nebuchadnezzar's narrative. Pride rewrites history to exclude divine involvement.

---

3. God's Warning: Mercy Before Discipline

Unlike Pharaoh, Nebuchadnezzar received **advance warning**. God did not ambush him with judgment; He appealed to him through a troubling dream.

Daniel faithfully interpreted the dream and issued a clear call to repentance:

"Break off thy sins by righteousness, and thine iniquities by shewing mercy to the poor."
— Daniel 4:27

This verse reveals God's heart. Discipline was **conditional**, not inevitable. Repentance could have altered the outcome.

The delay of twelve months between the warning and the judgment demonstrates divine patience. God gave Nebuchadnezzar time to humble himself.

Pride ignored the warning.

4. Divine Discipline Defined: Correction, Not Condemnation

When judgment finally came, it was severe but purposeful.

"They shall drive thee from men, and thy dwelling shall be with the beasts of the field."
— Daniel 4:32

Nebuchadnezzar lost:

- His throne
- His dignity
- His sanity

Yet he did not lose his life.

This distinction matters. Discipline is not annihilation. It is **intervention designed to restore alignment**.

The writer of Hebrews explains:

"For whom the Lord loveth he chasteneth."
— Hebrews 12:6

Nebuchadnezzar's humiliation was evidence not of abandonment, but of divine concern.

---

5. Humiliation as a Pathway to Humility

For seven years, Nebuchadnezzar lived like an animal. The king who exalted himself above men was reduced below them.

This humiliation reversed pride's distortion. Pride elevates self above reality. Humiliation restores truth.

"Till thou know that the most High ruleth in the kingdom of men."
— Daniel 4:32

God's objective was not suffering—it was **knowledge of sovereignty**.

Humility is often learned when illusion collapses.

6. The Turning Point: Recognition of God's Authority

The restoration of Nebuchadnezzar began with a single act: **acknowledgment**.

"And at the end of the days I Nebuchadnezzar lifted up mine eyes unto heaven."
— Daniel 4:34

This upward gaze symbolized surrender. Pride looks inward. Humility looks upward.

Immediately, understanding returned:

"And mine understanding returned unto me."
— Daniel 4:34

Restoration followed recognition.

---

7. Praise Replaces Pride

Nebuchadnezzar's transformation was not superficial. His confession was theological, not emotional:

"All the inhabitants of the earth are reputed as nothing: and he doeth according to his will."
— Daniel 4:35

The king who once exalted himself now exalted God. Pride had been replaced with reverence.

True humility does not diminish leadership—it **redeems it**.

---

8. Restoration Without Resentment

Scripture records an extraordinary outcome:

"My reason returned unto me; and for the glory of my kingdom... my counsellors and my lords sought unto me."
— Daniel 4:36

Nebuchadnezzar was restored fully:

- His throne
- His honor

- His influence

God did not permanently disqualify him. He corrected him.

This reveals a vital truth:
God opposes pride but restores the humble.

---

9. Discipline Versus Destruction: A Theological Contrast

Comparing Pharaoh and Nebuchadnezzar is instructive:

- Pharaoh hardened himself and was destroyed
- Nebuchadnezzar humbled himself and was restored

The difference was not God's power, but **human response**.

Pride that resists correction leads to judgment.
Pride that yields under correction leads to restoration.

---

10. Lessons for Leaders and Believers

Nebuchadnezzar's story offers enduring lessons:

- Success is a spiritual test
- God warns before He disciplines
- Humiliation can be redemptive
- Restoration follows surrender

Leadership does not exempt anyone from accountability. But humility can preserve both calling and legacy.

Conclusion: The Mercy Hidden in Discipline

Nebuchadnezzar's story reveals a God who disciplines not to destroy, but to save. Pride was confronted, stripped, and replaced—not by annihilation, but by mercy.

This chapter teaches a powerful truth:
God's discipline is severe only because His purpose is restorative.

End-of-Chapter Reflection

1. Why is success often a greater spiritual test than hardship?
2. How does God demonstrate mercy even in severe discipline?
3. What role does humility play in restoration?
4. How does Nebuchadnezzar's response differ from Pharaoh's?
5. Where might God be warning you before discipline becomes necessary?

End-of-Chapter Prayer

Sovereign Lord, keep my heart humble in seasons of success. Teach me to heed Your warnings and submit to Your authority. Let discipline produce righteousness and restoration in my life. Amen.

CHAPTER NINE

WHEN RELIGION BECOMES DANGEROUS: THE PRIDE OF THE PHARISEES

Introduction: The Most Deceptive Form of Pride

Not all pride wears the face of rebellion. Some pride kneels, fasts, prays, quotes Scripture, and appears devout. This is the most dangerous form of pride, the kind that cloaks itself in righteousness. Religious pride is uniquely deceptive because it convinces its host that closeness to God is already secured, rendering repentance unnecessary.

Jesus confronted no group more forcefully than the Pharisees, not because they were immoral, but because they were **self-righteous**. Their sin was not lawlessness; it was **law-based arrogance**. They did not reject God openly; they replaced Him subtly, using religion as a means of self-exaltation.

This chapter examines how religion, when divorced from humility, becomes a weapon rather than a pathway, and why Jesus considered religious pride more dangerous than overt sin.

---

1. Who Were the Pharisees? Guardians Turned Gatekeepers

The Pharisees did not begin as villains. Historically, they arose during a period when Israel sought to preserve faithfulness to God's law amid foreign influence. Their original aim was admirable: to protect holiness, preserve Scripture, and promote obedience.

Yet over time, devotion drifted into **distortion**. What began as reverence for the law evolved into **reverence for self**.

Jesus acknowledged their diligence:

"The scribes and the Pharisees sit in Moses' seat."
— Matthew 23:2

But He immediately warned against imitation:

"Do not ye after their works: for they say, and do not."
— Matthew 23:3

Their authority was positional. Their hearts were misaligned.

2. The Core of Religious Pride: Moral Superiority

Religious pride expresses itself not in defiance of God, but in **comparison with others**.

Jesus exposes this posture through a parable:

"God, I thank thee, that I am not as other men are."
— Luke 18:11

This prayer reveals pride's most subtle language: gratitude that is actually contempt. The Pharisee did not thank God for mercy; he thanked God for **difference**.

Moral superiority replaces repentance. The need for grace disappears when sin is always externalized.

3. External Righteousness, Internal Corruption

Jesus' strongest rebukes were reserved for religious hypocrisy:

"Woe unto you, scribes and Pharisees, hypocrites! for ye make clean the outside of the cup and of the platter, but within they are full of extortion and excess."
— Matthew 23:25

The Pharisees mastered outward compliance but neglected inward transformation. Pride thrives on appearance because appearance is controllable; the heart is not.

Religion becomes dangerous when it prioritizes **visibility over vulnerability**.

4. Knowledge Without Love: Pride Inflated by Truth

The Pharisees knew Scripture extensively. Yet knowledge, when untempered by humility, inflated the ego rather than shaped the soul.

Paul later warned the church:

"Knowledge puffeth up, but charity edifieth."
— 1 Corinthians 8:1

Truth divorced from love becomes a weapon. The Pharisees used Scripture not to heal but to accuse, not to restore but to condemn.

Religious pride delights in being right—even when it is unloving.

---

5. Pride and the Misuse of Authority

Jesus accused the Pharisees of obstructing access to God:

"Ye shut up the kingdom of heaven against men."
— Matthew 23:13

This is a devastating indictment. Pride does not merely mislead the proud; it **blocks others**. When leaders use spirituality to elevate themselves, they turn faith into a barrier.

Religion becomes dangerous when it exists to preserve status rather than serve people.

---

6. Pride's Fear of Exposure

Despite their public confidence, the Pharisees were deeply threatened by Jesus. His authority did not come from position but from alignment with God.

"Never man spake like this man."
— John 7:46

Jesus exposed hearts rather than performances. Religious pride fears exposure because it depends on image. This fear fueled hostility, not repentance.

Pride prefers control over truth.

---

7. The Ultimate Irony: Rejecting God While Defending God

The greatest tragedy of religious pride is irony. The Pharisees, in defending God's law, **rejected God Himself**.

"Ye search the scriptures... and they are they which testify of me. And ye will not come to me."
— John 5:39–40

They knew Scripture but missed its fulfillment. Pride blinded them to the very One they claimed to serve.

Religion without humility can become a substitute for relationship with God.

8. Why Jesus Ate with Sinners

Jesus' openness to sinners contrasted sharply with His opposition to Pharisees.

"They that are whole need not a physician; but they that are sick."
— Luke 5:31

Sinners knew they were sick. The Pharisees believed they were healthy. Pride is more resistant to grace than sin because it denies the need for healing.

This explains a shocking reality: **overt sinners repented more readily than religious elites**.

9. Modern Echoes of Pharisaic Pride

Religious pride did not die with the Pharisees. It reappears whenever:

- Doctrine becomes identity
- Morality becomes currency
- Service becomes superiority
- Correctness replaces compassion

Pride flourishes wherever faith becomes performance.

10. The Cure Jesus Prescribed: Humility of Heart

Jesus' solution was not abandoning truth, but embracing humility:

"Learn of me; for I am meek and lowly in heart."
— Matthew 11:29

Humility does not dilute holiness - it protects it. Only humility keeps religion from becoming dangerous.

Conclusion: The Danger of Being Too Right to Repent

The Pharisees were not condemned for knowing too much, but for **repenting too little**. Their pride made repentance unnecessary and mercy offensive.

This chapter reveals a sobering truth:
The closer religion moves to self-exaltation, the farther it moves from God.

End-of-Chapter Reflection

1. Why is religious pride more dangerous than moral failure?
2. How does comparison fuel spiritual arrogance?
3. In what ways can truth be misused without love?
4. How does pride turn religion into a barrier?
5. Where might humility be needed to keep faith authentic?

End-of-Chapter Prayer

Lord Jesus, deliver me from pride hidden in righteousness. Guard my heart from comparison and self-exaltation. Teach me to walk humbly, love deeply, and repent quickly. Amen.

CHAPTER TEN

**PRIDE, GIFTS, AND GRACE:

WHY GOD RESISTS THE PROUD BUT EMPOWERS THE HUMBLE**

Introduction: When Giftedness Outpaces Character

One of the most dangerous misunderstandings in spiritual life is the belief that **giftedness equals approval**. Scripture repeatedly exposes this assumption as false. God gives gifts freely, often generously, and sometimes astonishingly. Yet the presence of gifts does not imply the presence of humility, nor does it guarantee alignment with God's heart.

Many have mistaken ability for anointing, success for endorsement, and visibility for favor. Pride thrives in such confusion. It feeds on applause, influence, and effectiveness while quietly eroding character. The result is a paradox seen throughout Scripture and history: **people richly gifted yet spiritually resisted**.

This chapter confronts a hard truth: God may use the proud, but He does not empower them. He may allow gifts to function, but He withholds grace from hearts that exalt themselves. To understand why, we must distinguish between **gifts and grace**, and between **talent and character**.

---

1. Gifts Are Given; Grace Is Granted

The New Testament makes a clear distinction between gifts and grace.

Spiritual gifts are bestowed by God's sovereign choice:

"But the manifestation of the Spirit is given to every man to profit withal."
— 1 Corinthians 12:7

Gifts are not earned. They are not rewards for holiness. They are expressions of God's generosity and purpose.

Grace, however, operates differently.

"God resisteth the proud, but giveth grace unto the humble."
— James 4:6

Grace is not merely a gift; it is **a relational empowerment**. Grace flows toward humility because humility preserves alignment. Pride disrupts that alignment and therefore blocks grace.

A person may possess gifts without grace. But no one can fulfill purpose without grace.

---

2. The Purpose of Gifts: Service, Not Status

Scripture defines the purpose of spiritual gifts clearly:

"Even so minister the same one to another, as good stewards of the manifold grace of God."
— 1 Peter 4:10

Gifts are entrusted for service. Pride corrupts this purpose by transforming gifts into identity markers. Instead of serving others, gifts become tools for self-definition and elevation.

Pride says:

- *My gift distinguishes me*
- *My gift validates me*
- *My gift entitles me*

Humility says:

- *My gift serves others*
- *My gift is entrusted*
- *My gift points beyond me*

Where pride reassigns ownership of gifts, grace withdraws.

---

3. Why God Resists the Proud

The phrase *"God resisteth the proud"* is among the most sobering statements in Scripture. The Greek term used implies **active opposition**, not passive disapproval. God sets Himself against pride because pride is not a weakness—it is a rival posture.

Pride competes with God for:

- Glory
- Authority
- Trust
- Dependence

"Let him that glorieth glory in the Lord."
— 1 Corinthians 1:31

When a person glories in self, God's glory is displaced. Grace cannot operate where God's glory is redirected.

God's resistance to pride is therefore protective, not petty. Pride would destroy the person if left unchecked.

---

4. Character: The Container of Grace

Character determines capacity. Gifts determine function. Grace sustains both.

Jesus taught this principle through parable:

"No man putteth new wine into old bottles."
— Luke 5:37

Grace is the "new wine." Character is the container. Pride cracks the container. Humility strengthens it.

A gifted person without character may impress crowds, but he cannot sustain calling. Eventually, pressure exposes posture.

---

5. Saul, Samson, and Judas: Gifts Without Grace

Scripture provides sobering examples of gifted individuals who lacked sustaining grace.

Saul

- Gifted with leadership
- Empowered by the Spirit

- Yet resisted correction

Pride led to rejection.

Samson

- Endowed with supernatural strength
- Yet governed by appetite and self-indulgence

Gift remained; grace withdrew.

Judas

- Chosen as an apostle
- Empowered to heal and preach

Yet pride and self-interest destroyed him.

These cases reveal a frightening reality: **gifts can operate even when hearts are misaligned**. But grace will not remain where pride dominates.

---

6. Paul: A Model of Giftedness Anchored in Humility

Paul was among the most gifted individuals in the New Testament. Yet he consciously guarded against pride.

"And lest I should be exalted above measure... there was given to me a thorn in the flesh."
— 2 Corinthians 12:7

Paul interpreted limitation as mercy. He understood that unchecked pride would sabotage his calling.

"My grace is sufficient for thee."
— 2 Corinthians 12:9

Grace does not remove weakness; it redeems it. Humility allows weakness to coexist with power.

7. The Deception of Effectiveness

Effectiveness is not evidence of approval. God may still accomplish His purposes through flawed vessels, but that does not imply personal alignment.

Jesus issued a sobering warning:

"Many will say to me in that day, Lord, Lord, have we not prophesied...?"
— Matthew 7:22

Activity without intimacy is possible. Ministry without submission is possible. Pride often hides behind results.

Grace is measured not by output, but by obedience.

---

8. Humility: The Gateway to Empowerment

Humility does not deny gifting; it **submits gifting to God**.

"Humble yourselves therefore under the mighty hand of God, that he may exalt you in due time."
— 1 Peter 5:6

Exaltation is God's responsibility. Humility preserves timing. Pride rushes process and sabotages preparation.

God empowers the humble because humility keeps authority aligned with purpose.

---

9. Grace and Growth: Why Humble People Mature

Grace accelerates growth. Humble people learn quickly because they remain teachable.

"Surely he scorneth the scorners: but he giveth grace unto the lowly."
— Proverbs 3:34

Pride stagnates growth by resisting correction. Humility invites refinement.

Character develops where humility reigns.

10. Cultivating Humility in a Gifted Life

Scripture offers practical safeguards:

- Regular repentance
- Submission to accountability
- Embracing correction
- Serving quietly
- Giving glory to God

Humility must be cultivated intentionally, especially where gifts are strong.

Conclusion: Gifts Impress, Grace Sustains

Gifts may open doors, but grace keeps them open. Talent may attract attention, but humility preserves purpose. God does not oppose gifting—He opposes pride.

This chapter establishes a decisive truth:
God empowers the humble not because they are weak, but because they are safe vessels for His glory.

End-of-Chapter Reflection

1. Why do gifts sometimes operate without grace?
2. How can effectiveness mask spiritual misalignment?
3. What role does character play in sustaining calling?
4. Why does God actively resist pride?
5. How can humility be cultivated alongside gifting?

End-of-Chapter Prayer

Gracious God, guard my heart as You increase my gifts. Let humility anchor my calling and grace sustain my growth. May I never substitute effectiveness for obedience, or talent for surrender. Amen.

CHAPTER ELEVEN

THE SILENT KILLER: PRIDE IN GOOD WORKS

Introduction: When Doing Good Becomes Spiritually Dangerous

Not all pride announces itself through arrogance or defiance. Some pride works tirelessly. It serves faithfully. It gives generously. It labors sacrificially. And because it looks righteous, it often goes undetected—until it destroys the very purpose it claims to serve.

Pride in good works is among the most subtle and destructive forms of pride. It does not rebel openly against God; it attempts to **replace dependence on God with performance for God**. This pride believes that effort earns favor, sacrifice secures approval, and labor entitles reward. When unchecked, it transforms obedience into bargaining and service into self-justification.

This chapter examines how pride infiltrates service, how merit replaces mercy, and why religious labor—when divorced from humility—can become spiritually lethal.

1. The Deception of Merit: When Effort Replaces Grace

The human heart instinctively seeks control over acceptance. Pride offers a solution: *earn it*. If favor can be earned, then grace becomes unnecessary.

Scripture directly confronts this impulse:

"For by grace are ye saved through faith; and that not of yourselves: it is the gift of God: not of works, lest any man should boast."
— Ephesians 2:8–9

Boasting is the clue. Pride does not object to salvation; it objects to **undeserved salvation**. Pride prefers a system where contribution determines worth.

Good works are not wrong. Scripture commands them:

"For we are his workmanship, created in Christ Jesus unto good works."
— Ephesians 2:10

The danger lies not in works themselves, but in **the heart posture behind them**.

2. Cain and Abel: The First Religious Pride

The story of Cain and Abel is the earliest biblical illustration of pride in religious labor.

"And in process of time it came to pass, that Cain brought of the fruit of the ground an offering unto the LORD. And Abel... brought of the firstlings of his flock."
— Genesis 4:3–4

Both brought offerings. Both were religious. Yet God responded differently.

"And the LORD had respect unto Abel and to his offering: But unto Cain and to his offering he had not respect."
— Genesis 4:4–5

The issue was not agriculture versus livestock. It was **posture**. Abel brought an offering rooted in faith and dependence. Cain brought the product of his labor as **presentation of merit**.

Hebrews clarifies:

"By faith Abel offered unto God a more excellent sacrifice."
— Hebrews 11:4

Faith acknowledges dependence. Pride asserts sufficiency.

3. When Service Becomes Self-Justification

Cain's response to God's rejection is revealing:

"And Cain was very wroth, and his countenance fell."
— Genesis 4:5

Anger revealed entitlement. Cain believed his work obligated God. Pride always becomes offended when God does not validate effort.

God warned Cain graciously:

"If thou doest well, shalt thou not be accepted?"
— Genesis 4:7

The invitation was repentance, not performance. Cain rejected it. Pride prefers vindication over transformation.

This rejection of correction turned religious labor into resentment—and resentment into violence.

---

4. Pride in Sacrifice: When Cost Becomes Currency

Pride often measures righteousness by cost:

- How much was given
- How much was sacrificed
- How much was endured

Yet Scripture consistently rejects this calculus.

"To obey is better than sacrifice."
— 1 Samuel 15:22

Sacrifice without obedience is noise. Costliness does not compensate for misalignment. Pride equates pain with purity, suffering with sanctification.

God desires surrender more than sacrifice.

---

5. Charity and Recognition: Doing Good to Be Seen

Jesus directly addressed pride in charitable acts:

"Take heed that ye do not your alms before men, to be seen of them."
— Matthew 6:1

The issue is not visibility; it is **motivation**. Pride performs righteousness for recognition. Humility practices righteousness for obedience.

Jesus' warning is severe:

"They have their reward."
— Matthew 6:2

Recognition replaces reward when pride governs service.

6. The Labor Trap: When Ministry Becomes Identity

Religious labor becomes dangerous when it becomes identity.

"Martha, Martha, thou art careful and troubled about many things."
— Luke 10:41

Martha was serving Jesus—yet Jesus corrected her. Why? Because service had displaced devotion. Pride was not her arrogance, but her **self-importance in labor**.

Service that disconnects from intimacy breeds frustration, comparison, and resentment.

7. The Older Brother: Pride That Resents Grace

Jesus' parable of the prodigal son reveals pride hidden in obedience.

"Lo, these many years do I serve thee... yet thou never gavest me a kid."
— Luke 15:29

The older brother's words expose transactional righteousness. He served for reward, not relationship. Grace offended him because it disrupted his merit-based system.

Pride resents grace when grace undermines entitlement.

8. Religious Labor Without Love

Paul issues a sobering warning:

"Though I bestow all my goods to feed the poor... and have not charity, it profiteth me nothing."
— 1 Corinthians 13:3

Service without love profits nothing spiritually. Pride can fuel generosity, activism, and sacrifice—yet leave the heart unchanged.

Love humbles. Pride counts.

9. Why Pride Loves Good Works

Good works offer pride a respectable hiding place. Unlike blatant sin, religious labor earns applause. Pride prefers environments where effort is celebrated and motive is ignored.

But Scripture insists that **God examines the heart**.

"Man looketh on the outward appearance, but the LORD looketh on the heart."
— 1 Samuel 16:7

---

10. The Antidote: Grace-Driven Obedience

The solution is not abandoning good works but grounding them in grace.

"Let us have grace, whereby we may serve God acceptably."
— Hebrews 12:28

Grace-driven obedience:

- Serves without entitlement
- Gives without comparison
- Sacrifices without resentment
- Obeys without bargaining

Humility keeps service aligned.

Conclusion: When Good Works Kill the Soul

This chapter exposes a hard truth:
Good works can become deadly when they replace grace.

Cain's tragedy was not irreligion, but prideful religion. When service becomes a means of self-justification, it poisons worship, fractures relationships, and resists correction.

God does not reject good works—He rejects **prideful hearts behind them**.

End-of-Chapter Reflection

1. How can good works subtly replace dependence on grace?
2. What does Cain's offering reveal about motive and posture?
3. How does pride turn sacrifice into entitlement?
4. In what ways can service become identity rather than obedience?
5. How can love and humility safeguard religious labor?

End-of-Chapter Prayer

Gracious Father, cleanse my service of pride. Deliver me from striving to earn what You freely give. Let my obedience flow from love, my sacrifice from surrender, and my labor from humility. Amen.

CHAPTER TWELVE

CHRIST THE HUMBLE KING:

VOLUNTARY HUMILITY, THE CROSS, AND EXALTATION THROUGH OBEDIENCE**

Introduction: The Kingdom That Runs Opposite to Pride

If pride is the root of rebellion, then Jesus Christ is the root of restoration. Every chapter before this has exposed pride's destructive power—its cosmic origin, its human expression, its generational reach, and its religious disguises. Now Scripture brings us to the decisive contrast. In Christ, we do not merely see humility taught; we see humility **embodied**.

The Christian faith does not confront pride primarily with instruction, but with **incarnation**. God answered humanity's self-exaltation not by asserting greater dominance, but by **descending**. Where Adam grasped, Christ released. Where Lucifer exalted himself, Christ emptied Himself. Where pride sought a throne, humility chose a cross.

This chapter examines Christ as the **Humble King**, whose voluntary self-emptying (kenosis) overturned pride's logic and redefined greatness forever.

---

1. Philippians 2: The Most Radical Vision of Humility

Paul introduces his teaching on humility not with command alone, but with Christological revelation:

"Let this mind be in you, which was also in Christ Jesus."
— Philippians 2:5

Humility is not merely an ethic; it is a **mindset grounded in Christ's identity and actions**. Paul then unfolds one of the most profound passages in all of Scripture.

"Who, being in the form of God, thought it not robbery to be equal with God."
— Philippians 2:6

This statement affirms Christ's full divinity. Jesus did not lack status. He did not strive for equality with God—He already possessed it. His humility did not arise from inferiority, but from **security**.

True humility flows from knowing who you are before God.

---

2. Kenosis: What It Means—and What It Does Not Mean

Paul continues:

"But made himself of no reputation, and took upon him the form of a servant."
— Philippians 2:7

The Greek word *kenōsis* means "to empty." This does **not** mean Christ emptied Himself of divinity. He emptied Himself of **privilege**, **status**, and **rights**.

Kenosis is not self-denial in essence, but self-renunciation in posture.

Christ did not cease to be God; He chose not to **clutch** His divine prerogatives. Pride grasps. Humility releases.

This stands in direct contrast to Adam:

"Ye shall be as gods."
— Genesis 3:5

Adam reached upward in pride. Christ stepped downward in humility.

---

3. Incarnation as an Act of Humility

Paul emphasizes that Christ did not merely appear human:

"And was made in the likeness of men."
— Philippians 2:7

The incarnation itself was an act of humility. The Creator entered creation. The eternal stepped into time. The sovereign embraced dependence.

Jesus accepted:

- Hunger
- Fatigue
- Rejection
- Limitation

This was not forced upon Him.

"No man taketh it from me, but I lay it down of myself."
— John 10:18

Voluntary humility is humility at its purest.

---

4. Obedience: The Core of Christ's Humility

Paul identifies obedience as the defining expression of Christ's humility:

"He humbled himself, and became obedient unto death."
— Philippians 2:8

Obedience is humility in action. Jesus did not merely feel humble—He **submitted**.

This obedience was not selective. It was total.

"Not my will, but thine, be done."
— Luke 22:42

Where pride insists on self-determination, humility yields to God's will—even when it leads through suffering.

---

5. The Cross: The Ultimate Contradiction of Pride

Paul intensifies the statement:

"Even the death of the cross."
— Philippians 2:8

The cross was not only painful, it was humiliating. It was reserved for criminals, slaves, and rebels. It represented public shame, weakness, and disgrace.

Pride avoids shame at all costs. Christ embraced it.

"Who for the joy that was set before him endured the cross, despising the shame."
— Hebrews 12:2

Jesus redefined victory. Triumph came not through dominance, but through surrender.

6. Humility Without Resentment

Christ's humility was not bitter. He did not submit reluctantly.

"When he was reviled, reviled not again."
— 1 Peter 2:23

There was no self-pity, no vindictiveness, no self-defense. Pride demands justification. Humility entrusts judgment to God.

Jesus' silence before His accusers was not weakness—it was **authority under control**.

---

7. Exaltation: God's Response to Humility

Philippians does not end with humiliation.

"Wherefore God also hath highly exalted him."
— Philippians 2:9

Exaltation followed humility. The pattern is consistent throughout Scripture:

- Descent precedes ascent
- Surrender precedes authority
- Obedience precedes glory

Christ did not exalt Himself. God exalted Him.

"That at the name of Jesus every knee should bow."
— Philippians 2:10

What pride sought illegitimately, humility received legitimately.

---

8. The Name Above Every Name

God's exaltation of Christ was comprehensive:

- Universal authority
- Universal recognition
- Universal confession

"And that every tongue should confess that Jesus Christ is Lord."
— Philippians 2:11

The confession "Jesus is Lord" is the ultimate defeat of pride. It declares submission—not merely admiration.

---

9. Christ Versus Adam: Two Paths, Two Outcomes

Paul contrasts Adam and Christ elsewhere:

"For as by one man's disobedience many were made sinners, so by the obedience of one shall many be made righteous."
— Romans 5:19

Adam grasped and fell.
Christ released and rose.

Pride loses what it seeks.
Humility receives what it does not demand.

---

10. Implications for Believers and Leaders

Paul's exhortation is clear:

"Let this mind be in you."
— Philippians 2:5

Christ's humility is not merely to be admired—it is to be **imitated**.

This has practical implications:

- Leadership rooted in service
- Authority exercised through submission
- Identity secured in God, not position
- Obedience valued above recognition

Christian leadership is cruciform—it takes the shape of the cross.

11. Why Humility Is the Only Safe Power

Christ proves that humility is not weakness—it is the **only posture God entrusts with lasting authority.**

Power without humility corrupts.
Humility sanctifies power.

This is why God opposes pride and empowers the humble. Humility keeps authority aligned with God's glory.

Conclusion: The Throne Is Reached Through the Cross

Christ did not bypass the cross to reach the throne. The cross **was the pathway**.

This chapter establishes the final and decisive truth:
Humility is not the denial of greatness; it is the road to it.

In Christ, pride's logic is shattered forever.

End-of-Chapter Reflection

1. Why does true humility require security rather than insecurity?
2. How does Christ's humility contrast with Adam's pride?
3. What does kenosis teach about releasing privilege?
4. Why does God exalt those who do not exalt themselves?
5. How can Christ's humility reshape leadership and service today?

End-of-Chapter Prayer

Lord Jesus, teach me Your way of humility. Deliver me from the desire to exalt myself. Shape my life by obedience, surrender, and trust, that God may be glorified through me. Amen.

CHAPTER THIRTEEN

RESTORING WHAT PRIDE HAS DESTROYED:

REPENTANCE, BROKENNESS, AND THE REBUILDING OF PURPOSE**

Introduction: The Possibility of Restoration

If pride were only destructive and never redeemable, this book would end in despair. But Scripture does not leave us there. From Genesis to Revelation, the God who resists the proud is also the God who **restores the humble**. Pride destroys alignment, fractures relationships, and derails purpose; repentance restores alignment, heals fractures, and rebuilds what was lost.

Restoration is not denial of damage. It is not the erasing of consequences. It is the gracious work of God whereby a broken life is reoriented toward its original design. This chapter explores how God restores what pride has destroyed—through repentance that goes beyond regret, brokenness that opens the heart to grace, and a rebuilding process that places purpose back on a foundation of humility.

---

1. Repentance: More Than Regret

Repentance is often misunderstood as emotional sorrow. Scripture defines it far more deeply. Repentance (*metanoia*) is a **change of mind and direction**—a decisive turning from self-rule to God-rule.

Paul distinguishes regret from repentance:

"For godly sorrow worketh repentance to salvation not to be repented of: but the sorrow of the world worketh death."
— 2 Corinthians 7:10

Worldly sorrow mourns consequences. Godly repentance confronts posture. Pride regrets being caught; repentance confesses being wrong. Pride explains, repentance surrenders.

David's response after his sin reveals true repentance:

"Against thee, thee only, have I sinned."
— Psalm 51:4

Repentance begins when the heart stops defending itself and starts agreeing with God.

---

2. Brokenness: The Doorway to Grace

Brokenness is not humiliation imposed from outside; it is **surrender embraced from within**. Brokenness acknowledges dependence and relinquishes control.

Scripture gives a promise God never violates:

"A broken and a contrite heart, O God, thou wilt not despise."
— Psalm 51:17

Pride resists breaking because breaking feels like loss. In reality, brokenness is the loss of illusion. It is the moment self-sufficiency collapses and grace begins to flow.

Jesus affirmed this truth:

"Blessed are the poor in spirit: for theirs is the kingdom of heaven."
— Matthew 5:3

The kingdom is not given to the impressive, but to the dependent.

---

3. Grace: The Power That Rebuilds

Grace does more than forgive; it **reconstructs**. Forgiveness clears the ground. Grace rebuilds on it.

Peter writes:

"God resisteth the proud, but giveth grace unto the humble."
— 1 Peter 5:5

Notice the direction of grace—it flows *to* humility. Grace is not earned by humility; it is **released by it**. Where pride collapses, grace accelerates restoration.

Paul's testimony illustrates grace's rebuilding power:

"By the grace of God I am what I am."
— 1 Corinthians 15:10

Grace did not erase Paul's past; it redeemed it.

4. Biblical Portraits of Restoration

A. David: From Collapse to Continued Calling

David's pride led to moral failure, yet repentance preserved his calling. Though consequences followed, purpose was not canceled.

"Restore unto me the joy of thy salvation."
— Psalm 51:12

God restored David's intimacy, leadership, and legacy—not because David was flawless, but because he was **responsive**.

B. Peter: Failure Redeemed Through Humility

Peter's denial was public and humiliating. Yet his tears marked the beginning of restoration.

"And Peter went out, and wept bitterly."
— Luke 22:62

Jesus did not shame Peter; He recommissioned him:

"Feed my sheep."
— John 21:17

Grace rebuilt Peter into a pillar of the church.

C. Nebuchadnezzar: Authority Restored After Humility

As seen earlier, Nebuchadnezzar's restoration followed acknowledgment of God's sovereignty.

"Those that walk in pride he is able to abase."
— Daniel 4:37

Humility reopened the door to authority.

5. Rebuilding Purpose: Process, Not Instant Repair

God restores purpose, but rarely without process. Restoration is deliberate. It reshapes foundations before rebuilding structure.

Isaiah describes this work:

"And they that shall be of thee shall build the old waste places."
— Isaiah 58:12

God rebuilds on humility, not on reclaimed pride. Restored purpose is often deeper, wiser, and more anchored than the original.

What pride builds quickly; grace rebuilds carefully.

---

6. Guarding Restored Life

Restoration is not the end of vulnerability; it is the beginning of vigilance.

Scripture warns:

"Let him that thinketh he standeth take heed lest he fall."
— 1 Corinthians 10:12

The restored heart must be guarded by:

- Ongoing humility
- Accountability
- Gratitude
- Teachability
- Dependence on grace

Restoration teaches dependence. Pride reintroduces independence.

---

7. The Community Dimension of Restoration

God often restores individuals within community. Confession, counsel, and accountability protect humility.

James instructs:

"Confess your faults one to another and pray one for another."
— James 5:16

Isolation feeds pride. Community nurtures humility.

8. Restoration and Calling: Purpose Refined, Not Replaced

God does not restore prideful ambition; He restores **redeemed purpose**. Calling often returns with deeper compassion and clearer dependence.

"For the gifts and calling of God are without repentance."
— Romans 11:29

God's commitment to purpose is unwavering. What changes is the posture of the one called.

9. Living the Restored Life

A restored life bears distinct marks:

- Gratitude instead of entitlement
- Service instead of self-promotion
- Obedience instead of control
- Worship instead of self-glory

Restoration is evidenced not by regained status, but by **humility sustained**.

Conclusion: Pride Falls, Grace Raises

This book has traced pride from heaven's rebellion to human collapse, from leadership failure to religious arrogance. It now ends with hope: **pride does not have the final word**.

"Humble yourselves therefore under the mighty hand of God, that he may exalt you in due time."
— 1 Peter 5:6

God restores what pride destroys—not by bypassing humility, but by passing through it. Brokenness invites grace. Grace rebuilds purpose. And purpose, once restored, glorifies God rather than self.

Final End-of-Chapter Reflection

1. What distinguishes repentance from regret in your own life?
2. How does brokenness open the door to grace?
3. Which biblical restoration story speaks most deeply to you?
4. What safeguards are necessary to protect restored purpose?
5. How can humility be sustained beyond restoration?

Final Prayer of Surrender

Merciful Father, I lay down every trace of pride before You. Restore what has been broken, heal what has been wounded, and rebuild my life according to Your purpose. I choose humility, dependence, and obedience. Let my restored life bring glory to You alone. Amen.

PART A

FOREWORD (DELUXE EDITION)

Foreword

Why This Book Matters

Pride is one of the few sins Scripture treats not merely as dangerous, but as **foundationally destructive**. It is the sin that precedes rebellion, corrupts worship, poisons leadership, and resists grace itself. Yet it is also one of the least confronted—often tolerated, sometimes celebrated, and frequently misunderstood.

In *Pride and Purpose (Deluxe Edition)*, the author does not approach pride as a moral flaw to be corrected, but as a **spiritual posture that must be dismantled**. With theological clarity and pastoral sobriety, this work traces pride from its cosmic origin through its human manifestations, exposing how it distorts identity, fractures obedience, and derails divine purpose.

What distinguishes this book is its refusal to remain theoretical. Each chapter presses beyond explanation into **self-examination**, confronting pride where it hides most comfortably—in leadership, religion, service, gifting, and success. Scripture is not merely quoted; it is opened, weighed, and applied.

This is not a book written to entertain or affirm. It is written to awaken. It challenges readers to consider a sobering truth: God does not oppose weakness, ignorance, or failure—but He does oppose pride. And where pride is unaddressed, purpose is eventually lost.

Yet this book does not end in condemnation. It ends in hope. The same God who resists the proud restores the humble. Through repentance, brokenness, and grace, what pride has destroyed can be rebuilt on a firmer foundation.

This deluxe edition is not meant to be rushed. It is meant to be read prayerfully, slowly, and honestly. Those who do so will not merely gain insight, they will be invited into transformation.

PART B

PREFACE (DELUXE EDITION)

Preface

A Word to the Reader

This book was not written quickly, nor was it written casually. It was born out of years of reflection on Scripture, leadership, faith, and the repeated patterns that emerge whenever pride is allowed to operate unchecked—whether in individuals, institutions, or nations.

Pride is rarely acknowledged in its true form. More often, it disguises itself as confidence, competence, tradition, conviction, or even righteousness. Yet Scripture reveals pride as something far more serious: a **posture of independence from God**. It is this posture, not merely behavior that this book seeks to expose.

This deluxe edition exists because the subject demands depth. Pride cannot be dismantled with slogans. It requires sustained biblical engagement, honest examination, and theological clarity. Each chapter therefore builds upon the last, tracing pride from its origin in the heavens, through its entrenchment in human history, and ultimately to its defeat in Christ.

You will encounter familiar biblical figures in these pages—Lucifer, Adam, Saul, Pharaoh, Nebuchadnezzar, the Pharisees, and the apostles—but they are presented not as distant characters, but as mirrors. Their stories are included not to condemn them, but to instruct us.

This book is not written from a posture of superiority. Pride is not a problem "out there." It is a temptation common to all. If this book accomplishes its purpose, it will not leave the reader pointing fingers but searching hearts, including the author's.

Above all, this work is an invitation. An invitation to humility. An invitation to repentance. An invitation to restored purpose. God does not resist us to destroy us; He resists pride to save us.

Read with an open heart. Pause often. Pray honestly. And allow the Spirit of God to do what no book alone can do, reshape the heart.

About the Author

Elder Ehia Olu Akhabue is a devoted servant of God, a lifelong learner, and a man whose journey reflects a deep commitment to faith, excellence, and purposeful living. He is a cherished member of **RCCG Living Word Parish in Forney, Texas**, where he serves faithfully under the pastoral leadership of **Pastor Kolade Harrison,** a man anointed by God to preach and teach His Word with clarity and conviction. Elder Akhabue's spiritual walk is marked by humility, dedication, and a sincere desire to see believers grow in their relationship with God.

Before retiring, Elder Ehia Akhabue built a distinguished career as an educator and Information and Communication Technology professional. With expertise in **SAP (FICO)** and **MS SQL Database**, he contributed significantly to the development of systems, processes, and individuals throughout his professional life. His dual background as a teacher and ICT specialist reflects his passion for knowledge, structure, and the empowerment of others through learning.

Now retired and residing in Dallas, Texas, Elder Akhabue embraces a season of reflection, exploration, and renewed purpose. He enjoys traveling the world, immersing himself in new cultures, and appreciating the beauty of God's creation across continents. Reading has become one of his greatest joys in retirement, allowing him to continually expand his understanding of Scripture, history, and the world around him.

Elder Akhabue's writing is shaped by decades of spiritual growth, professional discipline, and personal reflection. His work carries the warmth of lived experience, the insight of a teacher, and the conviction of a man who has walked closely with God. He believes that every believer has a divine assignment and that spiritual maturity is cultivated through intentional living, consistent devotion, and a heart open to the leading of the Holy Spirit.

Through his words, Elder Akhabue seeks to inspire, encourage, and guide others toward a deeper, more meaningful walk with God - one rooted in truth, strengthened by faith, and expressed through a life of service.

Made in the USA
Coppell, TX
05 February 2026

71052177R10050